W9-CMO-116

BEYOND THE BATTLEFIELD

Hidden
Soldiers & Spies

ALLEN R. WELLS

Rourke
Educational Media

A Division of
Carson Dellosa Education

Before Reading: *Building Background Knowledge and Vocabulary*

Building background knowledge can help children process new information and build upon what they already know. Before reading a book, it is important to tap into what children already know about the topic. This will help them develop their vocabulary and increase their reading comprehension.

Questions and Activities to Build Background Knowledge:

1. Look at the front cover of the book and read the title. What do you think this book will be about?
2. What do you already know about this topic?
3. Take a book walk and skim the pages. Look at the table of contents, photographs, captions, and bold words. Did these text features give you any information or predictions about what you will read in this book?

Vocabulary: *Vocabulary Is Key to Reading Comprehension*

Use the following directions to prompt a conversation about each word.

- Read the vocabulary words.
- What comes to mind when you see each word?
- What do you think each word means?

Vocabulary Words:

- blockade
- enlist
- fugitive
- raid
- regiment
- transgender

During Reading: *Reading for Meaning and Understanding*

To achieve deep comprehension of a book, children are encouraged to use close reading strategies. During reading, it is important to have children stop and make connections. These connections result in deeper analysis and understanding of a book.

Close Reading a Text

During reading, have children stop and talk about the following:

- Any confusing parts
- Any unknown words
- Text to text, text to self, text to world connections
- The main idea in each chapter or heading

Encourage children to use context clues to determine the meaning of any unknown words. These strategies will help children learn to analyze the text more thoroughly as they read.

When you are finished reading this book, turn to the next-to-last page for **After-Reading Questions** and an **Activity**.

Table of Contents

Secret Spies

Harriet Tubman

Harriet Tubman is famous as the fearless leader who helped enslaved people escape slavery through the Underground Railroad. But did you know that she was also a military spy during the Civil War?

In 1862, Tubman was recruited as a spy for the Union Army as a result of her work with the Underground Railroad. She then recruited other former enslaved people to form a spy ring. Tubman was given a secret mission. She partnered with Colonel James Montgomery, and they planned a **raid** of plantations along the Combahee River. This made Tubman the first woman to ever lead a military mission in United States history.

raid (rayd): a sudden surprise attack on a place

Harriet Tubman

In June of 1863, Tubman and Montgomery set off on their mission. They used three boats to travel along the Combahee River to get to the plantations. Tubman guided the boats using the information she gained from her spy ring. When the signal was given, the enslaved people ran to shore so that Black troops could transport them to Union ships.

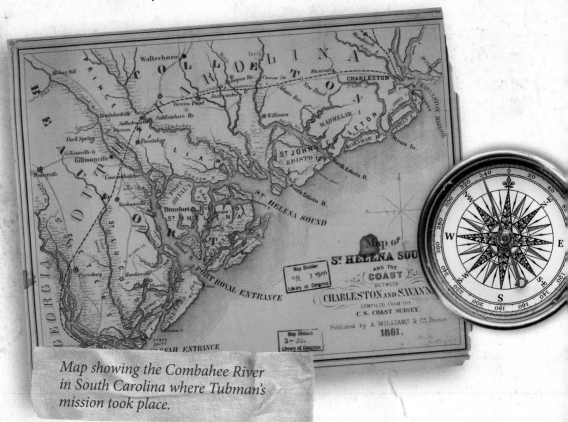

Map showing the Combahee River in South Carolina where Tubman's mission took place.

More than 700 people made it onto the boats and escaped slavery.

After the raid on the Combahee River, Tubman continued as a spy for the Union Army and was involved in other missions. Unfortunately, little is known about those missions.

Plantations burnt down as Tubman helped free enslaved people along the Combahee River.

Hercules Mulligan and Cato

In colonial New York, Hercules Mulligan was a tailor who catered to wealthy people, businessmen, and British officers. But when the Revolutionary War began in April 1775, Mulligan's access to British officers gave him the perfect opportunity to become a spy for General George Washington.

Hamilton

You might be familiar with Mulligan's friend from the popular musical! It was Alexander Hamilton who recommended Hercules Mulligan to serve as a spy for General Washington.

Mulligan outfitted the British officers, all while learning their secrets. Mulligan was able to predict their movements by asking when they needed their repaired uniforms.

A tailor from around Mulligan's time working in his shop.

If two or more officers stated the same date, he knew that's when they would be on the move. He would then relay the information to Cato, who was enslaved by Mulligan, and Cato delivered the messages to Washington.

Mulligan and Cato may have saved Washington's life. A British officer came to Mulligan for a coat very late at night. Mulligan asked why the officer needed a coat so late and so quickly. The officer told Mulligan that he had plans to capture Washington the following day. Mulligan relayed the information to Cato, who alerted Washington of the threat. Thanks to the information, Washington was safe.

After the war, Washington did not forget Mulligan's efforts. When Washington became president, he continued to shop in Mulligan's tailor shop, which made it famous. Although Cato played a significant role in the war efforts, little is known of his life after the Revolutionary War.

George Washington

James Armistead Lafayette

Born an enslaved person in the middle of the 1700s, James Armistead spent most of his life on a plantation in New Kent, Virginia. He left the plantation during the Revolutionary War when his enslaver, William Armistead, gave him permission to **enlist** in the Continental Army in 1781.

James Armistead was sent to serve under the Marquis de Lafayette's allied French forces. Lafayette decided to enlist James Armistead as a spy. James Armistead pretended to be a **fugitive** from slavery, spying on Americans for the British.

James Armistead Lafayette

enlist (en-LIST): to join the army, navy, or other armed forces

fugitive (FYOO-ji-tive): someone who is running away, especially from the law

James Armistead knew the terrain of Virginia well—
every river, hill, road, and passage. This made the
British trust him, and he was able to learn details
about British war plans that he could relay to Lafayette.

James Armistead played a major role in the surrender
of the British. He informed Washington and Lafayette
that 10,000 British troops were moving to Yorktown,
Virginia, a city located on a peninsula.

This allowed the generals to formulate a **blockade** preventing the troops from leaving the peninsula by land or sea. Trapped, the British surrendered on October 19, 1781. This major victory led to the end of the Revolutionary War.

The British surrender at Yorktown.

blockade (blah-KADE): the closing off of an area to keep people or supplies from going in or out

After the Revolutionary War, Americans celebrated freedom and the end of the war. But James Armistead had to return to a life of enslavement. Because he was a spy, he could not benefit from laws that freed enslaved people who fought in the war.

James Armistead went to the Virginia legislature multiple times to petition for his freedom but was denied. It wasn't until his friend, Lafayette, wrote a letter to congress on Armistead's behalf that he was freed.

A Name in Honor

On receiving his freedom, James Armistead added *Lafayette* to his name as a token of gratitude and testament to the bond that he and the French general shared.

Marquis de Lafayette

SURPRISING SOLDIERS

Deborah Sampson

It was 1782, in the midst of the Revolutionary War. Deborah Sampson disguised herself as a man and joined the Patriot forces under the name Robert Shurtleff. It is unclear why Sampson went to these lengths to join the war. One theory is that she had a strong sense of patriotism. Another theory is that she needed the payment promised to volunteer soldiers because she lived in poverty.

Sampson was to be part of the Light Infantry Troops. These troops were chosen because they were quick. They often had small, risky missions and were given fewer supplies. This is why they were called a "light" infantry.

Deborah Sampson

For two years, Sampson's identity as a woman was a secret. She had received multiple injuries and was even said to have been shot, but she rarely sought medical treatment for fear her secret would be discovered. It was not until she fell ill with a high fever that Sampson had to see a doctor and her identity was finally discovered.

Sampson received an honorable discharge for her courageous efforts in battle. She was the only woman to earn a full military pension for her contributions to the Revolutionary War.

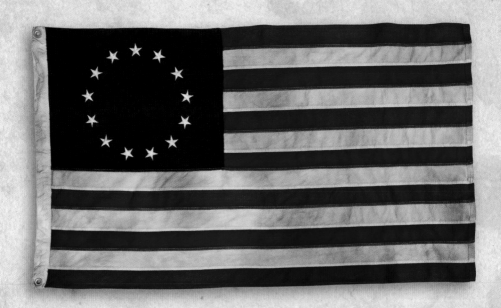

Deborah Sampson's gravestone in Sharon, Massachusetts. Additional monuments honoring Sampson are located near her grave.

DEBORAH,
SAMPSON,
GANNETT,
ROBERT SHURTLEFF
The Female Soldier
Service 1781 to 1783.

DEBORAH
SAMPSON
GANNETT

WOMAN SOLDIER IN THE WAR OF THE
REVOLUTION·ENLISTED UNDER THE NAME
OF ROBERT SHURTLEFF·SEVERAL YEARS
IN ACTIVE SERVICE·WOUNDED IN THE
BATTLE OF TARRYTOWN·HONORABLY
DISCHARGED IN 1783·PENSIONED BY
CONGRESS IN 1805

THIS TABLET IS PLACED HERE
BY REQUEST OF HER GRANDSON
GEORGE WASHINGTON GAY

A monument honoring Deborah Sampson in Sharon, Massachusetts.

Albert Cashier

Albert Cashier was born in Ireland. At birth, he was given a female sex assignment and given the name Jennie Hodgers. He always wore men's clothing, even before moving to the United States and enlisting in the army in 1862.

Cashier enlisted as a man in the Union Army during the Civil War. He was known by fellow soldiers as a brave fighter. One soldier recalled a specific story of Cashier's bravery on a dangerous mission. During a siege of the Confederate Fort Vicksburg, Cashier was sent behind enemy lines to gain information. He was captured by a Confederate soldier. Cashier escaped by taking the soldier's gun and running back to safety.

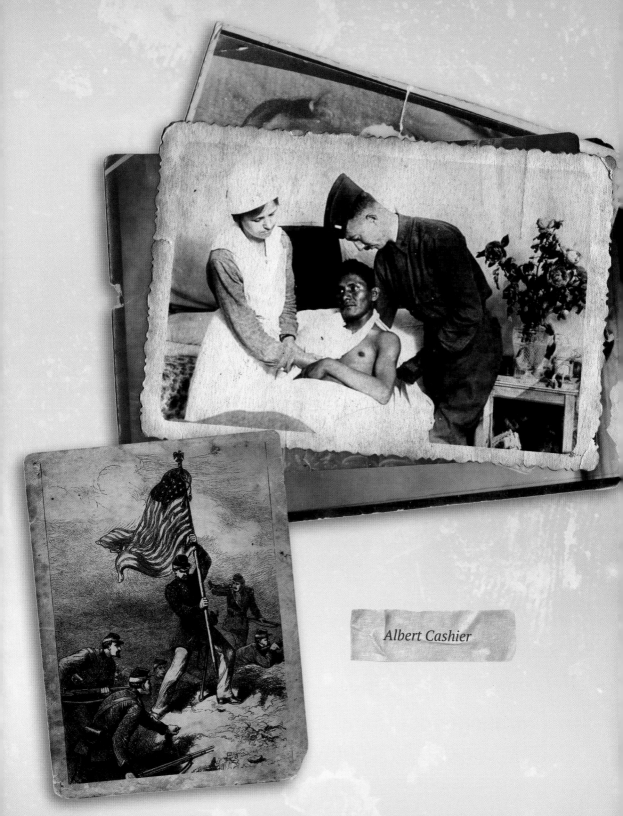

Albert Cashier

Cashier continued to live his life as a man even after the war was over. Though some who knew him knew his secret, it wasn't until he fell ill that it became widely known. When he had to be confined to a hospital, he was forced to live as a woman, which is said to have made his mental state worse and worse. Today, many scholars think of Cashier as **transgender**.

transgender (trans-JEN-dur): referring to a person whose gender identity is different from the sex they were assigned at birth

Albert Cashier with a fellow Civil War soldier.

HIDDEN FEMALE FLIGHT UNIT
The Night Witches

In June 1941, in the midst of World War II, the Soviet Union was invaded by Nazi Germany. This invasion was the largest invasion in history. The Soviet Union was outnumbered, and their enemies were better equipped, especially in the air.

Colonel Marina Raskova, a Soviet pilot, started receiving letters from Russian women who wanted to be involved in the war effort. Raskova convinced the military to allow women to have more active roles.

Raskova was charged with establishing three all-female air squads named the 588th Night Bomber **Regiment**. The squads were completely made up of women—the pilots, the commanders, and the mechanics.

Colonel Marina Raskova

regiment (REJ-uh-muhnt): a military unit consisting usually of two or more battalions

The regiment was given old equipment. The planes they flew were slow, unprotected, and couldn't carry very much weight. Because of this, the regiment only made bombing runs when it was dark. This way, they were harder to spot.

The planes were so small that they didn't show up on the radar of the enemy. But they were loud. To stay hidden, pilots would turn off their engines when they got close to their target.

Extraordinary Achievements

Despite the lack of resources and support, the Night Witches were able to complete around 30,000 bombing raids.

When they did this, the planes would make a "whooshing" sound that resembled a sweeping broom. That was the only way that the Germans would know they were coming. German soldiers started calling them the *Nachthexen* or "Night Witches." The regiment liked the name and started using it.

Raskova with two fellow pilots.

Memory Game

Look at the pictures. What do you remember reading on the pages where each image appeared?

Index

After-Reading Questions

1. How was Harriet Tubman recruited as a spy?

2. Who was Cato?

3. How did James Armistead gain the trust of the British while he was a spy?

4. Why was Albert Cashier sent behind enemy lines during the siege of Fort Vicksburg?

5. What does the term *Nachthexen* mean?

Activity

What are some of the qualities you think the soldiers and spies from this book have in common? For example, you might think they are all brave. Make a list of qualities. Are there any qualities on your list that you also have? Are there any that you would like to develop in yourself?

About the Author

Allen R. Wells loved researching and refamiliarizing himself with the hidden figures in this book. Allen admires their perseverance and determination to fight for what they believe. He writes wherever he finds inspiration. He lives in Atlanta, Georgia, where he works as a mechanical engineer and children's author.

www.rourkeeducationalmedia.com

PHOTO CREDITS: cover: eastern archive/ Shutterstock.com, FabrikaSimf/ Shutterstock.com, Alex Staroseltsev/ Shutterstock.com, Taigi/ Shutterstock.com, LiliGraphie/ Shutterstock.com; Inside Cover: DarkBird/ Shutterstock.com, Alex Staroseltsev/ Shutterstock.com, Taigi/ Shutterstock.com TOC: waku/ Shutterstock.com; TOC, page 32: TADDEUS/ Shutterstock.com; page 4, 8, 12, 18, 22, 26: ©DarkBird/ Shutterstock.com; page 4, 5: Here/ Shutterstock.com; page 5, 30: Photos.com/ Getty Images, National Archives and Records Administration, DarkBird/ Shutterstock.com; page 5, 6, 7, 9, 11, 13, 19, 21, 23, 27, 29: Picsfive/ Shutterstock.com; page 6-7, 14-15, 24-25, 30-31: DarkBird/ Shutterstock.com; page 6: Library of Congress, Geography and Map Division; Alex Staroseltsev/ Shutterstock.com; page 7: Picsfive/Shutterstock.com, Everett Collection/Newscom; page 8,16, 28: LiliGraphie/ Shutterstock.com; page 8, 30: 1000Photography / Shutterstock.com; page 9: whitemay/ Getty Images, Stephanie Frey/ Shutterstock.com, Ingrid Pakats / Shutterstock.com; page 10-11, 20-21, 26-27: DarkBird/ Shutterstock.com; page 11: DarkBird/ Shutterstock.com, GeorgiosArt/ Getty Images; page 12: Wicki58/ Getty Images, sozon/ Shutterstock.com; page 13: / DarkBird/ Shutterstock.com; page 13, 30: Everett Collection/ Shutterstock.com; page 14: Taigi/ Shutterstock.com, Library of Congress, Geography and Map Division; page 15, 19: DarkBird/ Shutterstock.com; page 15: pictore/ Getty Images; page 16: Skillman Library Special Collections and College Archives, Lafayette College; page 16-17, 28-29: photonova/ Shutterstock.com; page 17: caesart/ Shutterstock.com, traveler1116/ Getty Images; page 18-19: Olga_Z/ Getty Images; page 18: FlamingPumpkin/ Getty Images: page 19: Library of Congress Prints and Photographs Division; page 20: David Smart/ Shutterstock.com; page 21, 30: Wiki Commons; page 21: Digital Commonwealth, vav63/ Getty Images; page 23: duncan1890/ Getty Images, DarkBird/ Shutterstock.com; page 23-30: Abraham Lincoln Presidential Library and Museum, DarkBird/ Shutterstock.com; page 25: MBR/KRT/Newscom, DarkBird/ Shutterstock.com; page 26: 1008 / Shutterstock.com; page 27: warhistoryonline.com, DarkBird/ Shutterstock.com; page 28: zim286/ Getty Images; page 29, 30: migavia.com; page 29: malerapaso/ Getty Images

Edited by: Hailey Scragg
Cover and interior design by: Morgan Burnside

Library of Congress PCN Data

Hidden Soldiers and Spies / Allen R. Wells
 (Beyond the Battlefield)
 ISBN 978-1-73164-893-8 (hard cover)
 ISBN 978-1-73164-841-9 (soft cover)
 ISBN 978-1-73164-945-4 (e-Book)
 ISBN 978-1-73164-997-3 (ePub)
Library of Congress Control Number: 2021935286

Rourke Educational Media
Printed in the United States of America
01-1662111937